Curious George
Learns to Count
from 1 to 100

Published in the United States by HMH Books, an imprint of Houghton Mifflin
Harcourt Publishing Company. Originally published in hardcover in the United States by
Houghton Mifflin Company, an imprint of Houghton Mifflin Publishing Company, 2005.

Curious George ® is a registered trademark of Houghton Mifflin Harcourt Publishing Company.

The text of this book is set in Century Schoolbook and Eraser Dust.
Illustrated by Anna Grossnickle Hines.
Designed by Madeleine Budnick.

The Library of Congress has cataloged the hardcover edition as follows:
Curious George learns to count / illustrated in the style of
H. A. Rey by Anna Grossnickle Hines.
p. cm.
Summary: When Curious George learns to count to 100, he finds
that he can count almost anything, with some strange and unusual results.

[1. Monkeys—Fiction. 2. Counting.] I. Title: Curious George
counts to one hundred. II. Rey, H. A. (Hans Augusto), 1898–1977. III. Hines, Anna Grossnickle, ill.
PZ7.C9213635 2005
[E]—dc22
2004015766

ISBN: 978-0-618-47602-2 hardcover
ISBN: 978-0-547-13841-1 paperback

Manufactured in China
SCP 10 9 8 7 6

4500694706

Curious George

Learns to Count from 1 to 100

Illustrated in the style of H. A. Rey by Anna Grossnickle Hines

HMH Books
Houghton Mifflin Harcourt
Boston   New York

This is George. George was a good little monkey and always very curious. This morning George was curious about numbers. His friend, the man with the yellow hat, had been teaching him to count. Already George could count to five on one hand and ten on his two feet.

"Good job, George!" said his friend. "But you can count more than your fingers and toes. We're going to the Centennial Celebration today—it's our town's one hundredth birthday party. I'll bet you can find enough things to count all the way to one hundred!"

One hundred sounded
like a lot to George.

He was curious.
Could he really find one
hundred things to count?

First George counted his bed—**1**. Then he counted **2** blankets.
He tossed his pillows and counted **1, 2, 3**! He counted **4** legs
on his bed and **5** pull toys. What else could George count?

Why, there were lots of things in the toy box!

There were **6** toy boats,

7 cars,

8 trucks,

9 stuffed animals,

and **10** balls.

George followed one bouncing ball into his
friend's room. The man with the yellow hat was
getting dressed. George wanted to dress up, too!

He saw  hats to choose from,

12 ties,

13 socks,

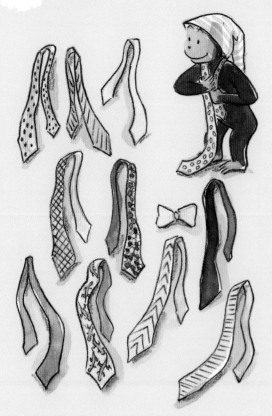

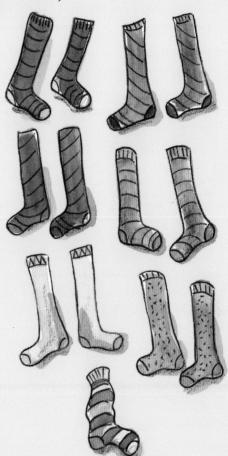

and **14** shoes,

Can you pick a pair of shoes for George? How does he look?

In the bathroom, George's friend had just finished brushing his teeth. "I'm going to make breakfast, George," he said. But George was still busy counting. He counted **15** blue tiles,

16 rubber ducks,

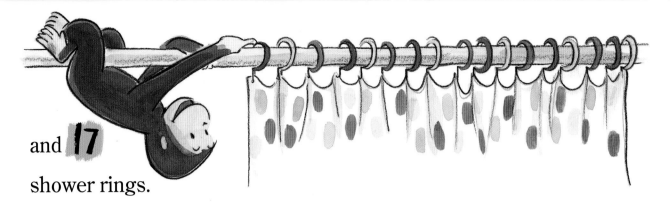

and **17**

shower rings.

It was fun to

count upside down!

Then George drew a surprise for his friend—

18

toothpaste

pictures.

In the kitchen, George found more things to count.

He stacked up **19** plates, **20** bowls, and **21** cups.

He arranged **22** straws,

23 napkins,

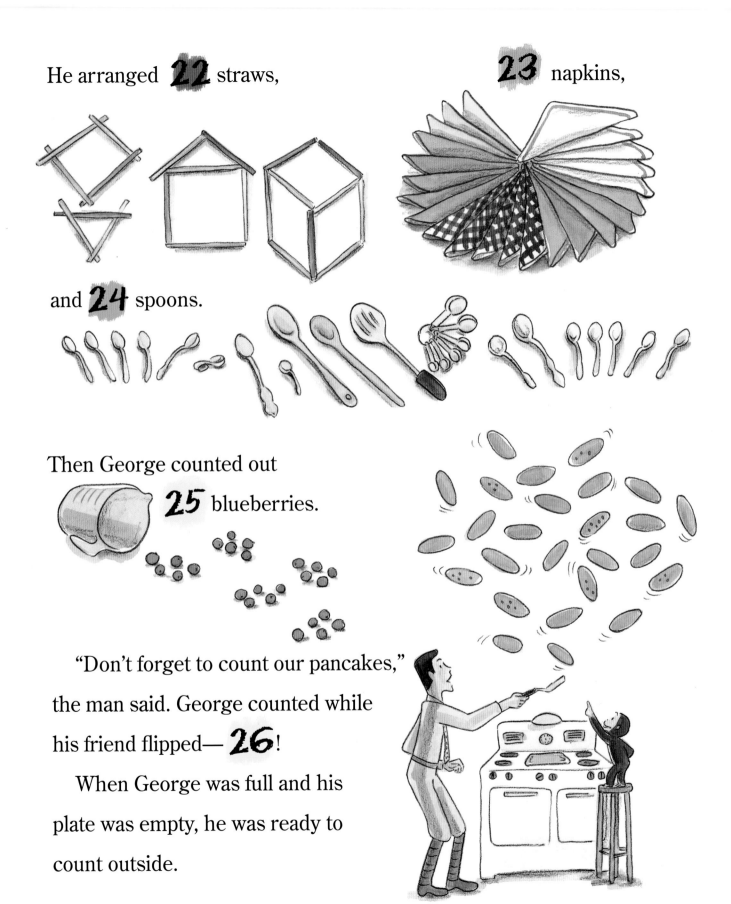

and **24** spoons.

Then George counted out **25** blueberries.

"Don't forget to count our pancakes," the man said. George counted while his friend flipped—**26**!

When George was full and his plate was empty, he was ready to count outside.

In the backyard George counted **27** clouds floating by—

and **28** apples on a tree.

Do you see the animals in the clouds? What other shapes can you find?

There was lots to do outside!

George played with **29** bugs

and gathered **30** acorns.

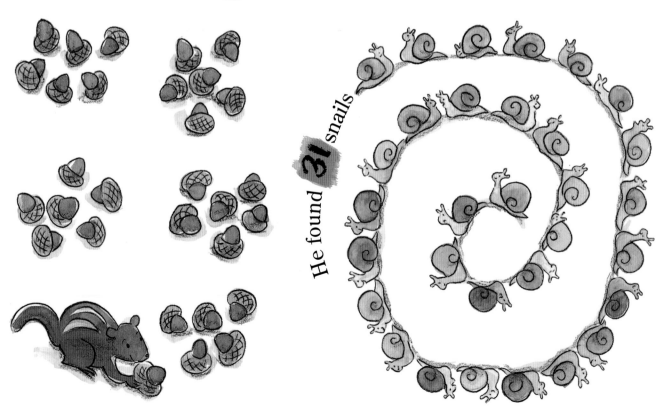

He found **31** snails

and arranged **32** sticks to create a design.

Next time you're outside, see what you can collect to make your own nature art. How many designs can you make?

Then George smelled the daisies—and he picked **33**!

Today's the day!
100 years!

Celebrate
100 YEARS
TODAY
in the Park

In his front yard George counted
34 noisy birds and **35** leaves blowing in the air. There was
something else in the air—a gust of wind scattered **36** letters with
colorful stamps! George counted as he helped pick them up.

"It's time to go to the Centennial Celebration, George," his friend
said. "Do you remember how to walk to town? You can lead the way."

George, curious as ever, took the long way from his house to town! As he walked, he counted **37** houses, **38** chimneys, and **39** trees. Can you follow George's path through his neighborhood?

Can you find a shorter way
from George's house to town?
How many buildings do you
see that are not houses?

ED'S GAS

TASTY MARKET

In town, George and his friend saw workers fixing up a building. There was a very tall ladder—and George could not resist! He scampered up **40** rungs past **41** windows.

What a view! From up on top of the ladder, George counted **42** people. One of them was his friend Betsy!

"Hi, George," Betsy said when he climbed down to see her. "Your friend told me you are learning to count."

Then George walked Betsy to her school.

"Why don't you come inside?" she asked him. "There are lots of things to count in here!"

Betsy was right. There were plenty of things to count in her classroom!

While George's friend talked to the teacher . . .

George counted **43** sparkly beads,

44 jars of paste,

and **45** crayons.

On the table **46** colorful feathers were laid out.

George was curious—what were they for?

Betsy's classmates were making hats and decorations for the Centennial Celebration. George wanted to make decorations, too.

In fact, he turned himself into a decoration!

Then George's new friends cleaned off **47** colored strips of paper—and a lot of glue!

"George is counting all the way to one hundred," Betsy said.

Susan said, "We can help! How about counting paperclips?"

She and her sister Sarah helped George find **48**.

"There are lots of books on the shelf," said Jimmy. They counted **49**.

"And states on the map," Henry added. He and George counted all 50.

All the students had lots of ideas, and
soon everyone was counting.

"Look at the art," Betsy said.
"We made different things,
but we can count all the art
together—**51**!"

On the wall was the alphabet.

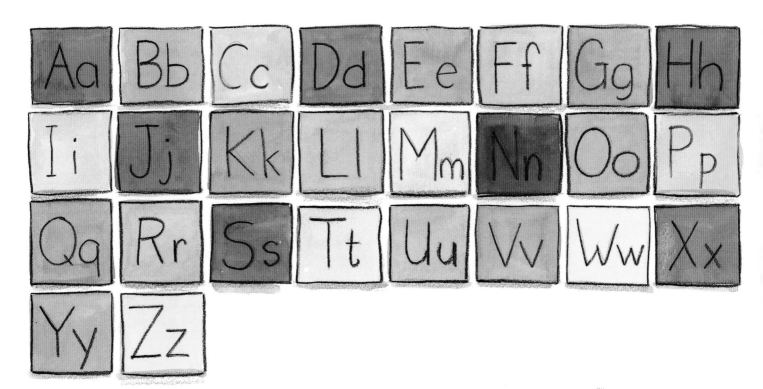

Together they counted **52** letters,
big and small.

George was excited to find **53** colored pencils. These were even better than toothpaste for drawing!

"We aren't allowed to write on the desks," the children told him, and they helped him clean up with **54** pink erasers.

Then they took out lots of paper . . .

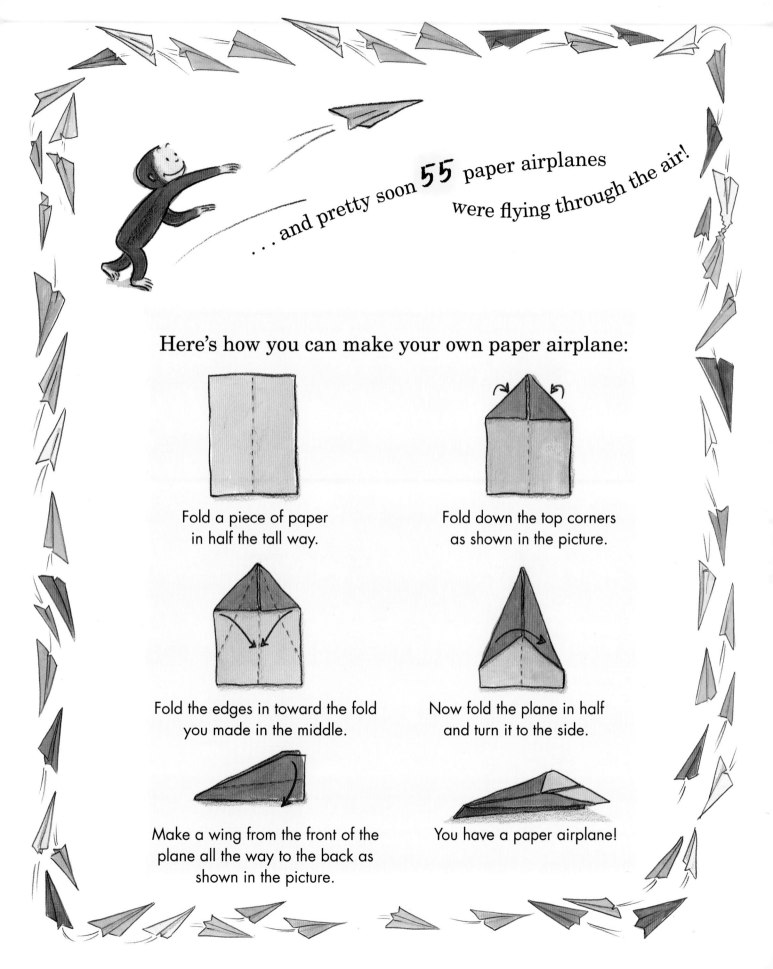

...and pretty soon **55** paper airplanes were flying through the air!

Here's how you can make your own paper airplane:

Fold a piece of paper
in half the tall way.

Fold down the top corners
as shown in the picture.

Fold the edges in toward the fold
you made in the middle.

Now fold the plane in half
and turn it to the side.

Make a wing from the front of the
plane all the way to the back as
shown in the picture.

You have a paper airplane!

George chased one of the paper airplanes past the aquarium.

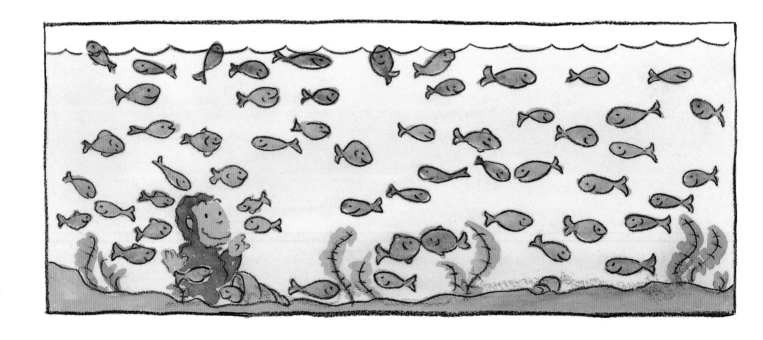

Now here was something to count—look at all the goldfish! George counted 56.

One of the airplanes landed on a cage.

"We have lots of class pets," Betsy told George. "And our mice just had babies!"

George couldn't wait to count them. But the mice would not keep still. It was hard to count them in their cages. Carefully, George lifted the latch . . .

There were **57** mice! And, boy, were they speedy!

When the mice were back in their cage, the teacher said, "I think it is time for us to go to the Centennial Celebration."

"I think we should go now, too," the man with the yellow hat said to George.

George waved goodbye to the children and counted **58** hands waving back.

A moment later the bell rang and everyone was on the move!

Then George counted **59** wheels.
He wanted to ride, too.

"You can borrow my bike, George," said Bill.

Ride on, George!

What's Maria giving to the man in the yellow hat? How many wheels will he be riding on?

Then George hopped on Bill's bike and pedaled away.
While he rode he counted **60** fence pickets.

and **61** dandelions.

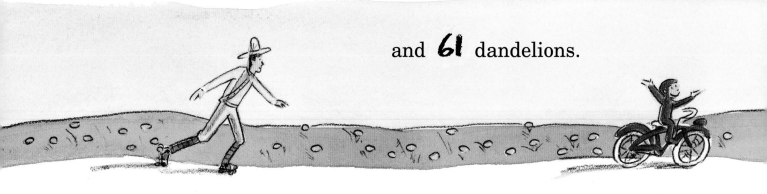

He blew **62** dandelion seeds.

And along the river George passed **63** ducks . . .

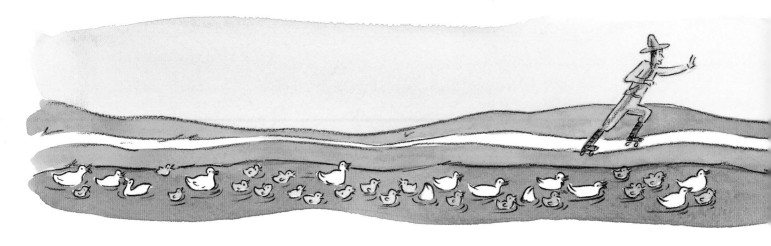

and **64** boats.

He counted **65** flags

and **66** bubbles floating in the air.

George was so busy counting, he forgot to watch where he was going.

He was surprised to look down the hill and see the Centennial Celebration in the park below! There were **67** colorful picnic blankets **68** striped tents, and **69** kites soaring in the breeze. George was excited to get closer. Seeing the picnics had made him hungry, and he was ready to get something to eat.

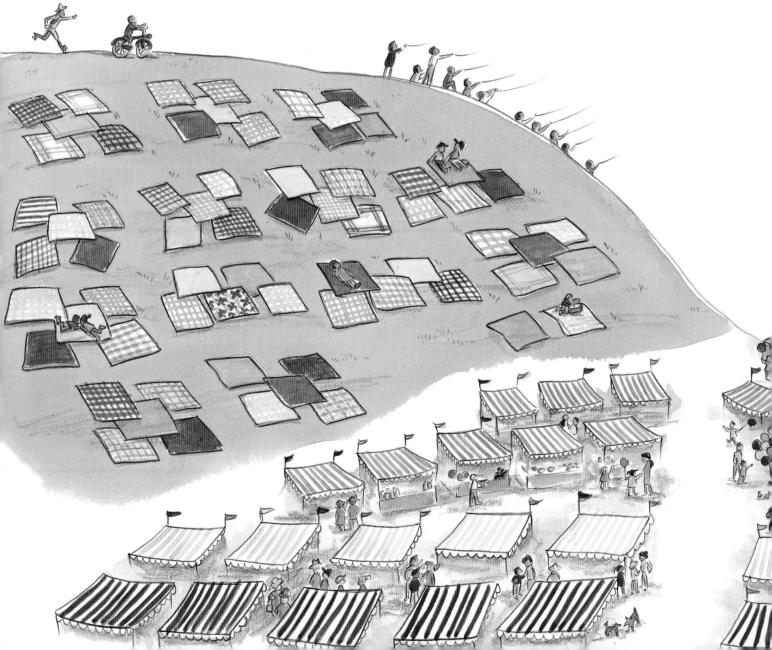

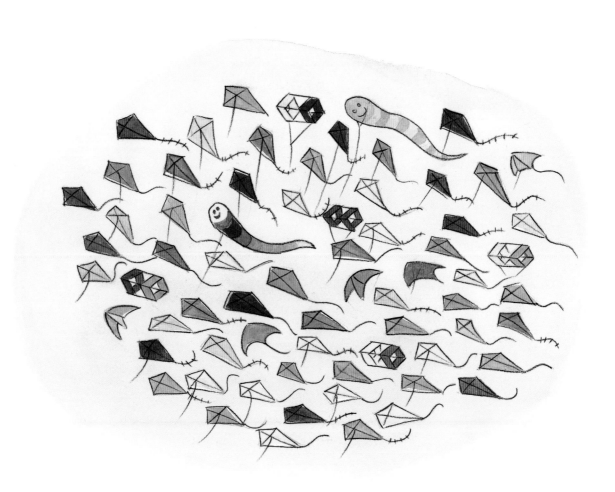

First George visited the farmer's market. Vegetables were piled high!

George counted **70** carrots,

71 peppers,

72 tomatoes,

and **73** pumpkin seeds.

oops!

The fruit looked as appealing as the vegetables . . . and tasted as good, too!

George counted **74** lemons,

LEMONADE

First, find 1 grownup to help you make this.

Combine
1/2 cup sugar
1/2 cup water

Heat in a pot until the sugar dissolves—but don't let it boil!

Add
6 cups room-temperature water
1 cup juice from lemons

Stir.
Pour over ice
and drink!

Just like a monkey. . .

75 bananas,

76 pears, and **77** grapes. He helped himself to some of each, and soon his tummy was full.

George had eaten and counted so many things, but he had not yet counted all the way to one hundred. George was curious. What else could he count? And what was that sound coming from across the street?

It was a parade! And it was time for the Centennial Celebration to begin! George's friends and neighbors had gathered to celebrate the one hundredth anniversary of their town. They were all lined up, clapping and cheering.

George climbed the lamppost for a better view.

What should he count first?

Can you find George?
Where did he get that hat?

As the parade marched by, George counted hats—there were **78**.

Which hats did Betsy and her friends make at school?

He counted all the pets— 79 .

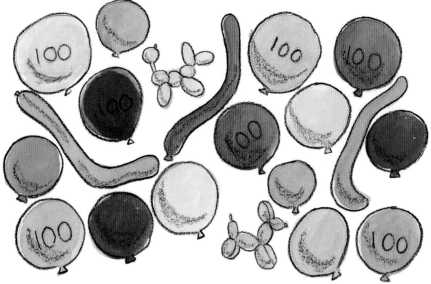

And balloons— **80** !

How many more things does he have to count to reach 100?

Mmmm! George followed good smells to the picnic blankets. If you were going on a picnic, what food would you pack?

George discovered **81** sandwiches,

82 pickles,

And **83** potato chips.

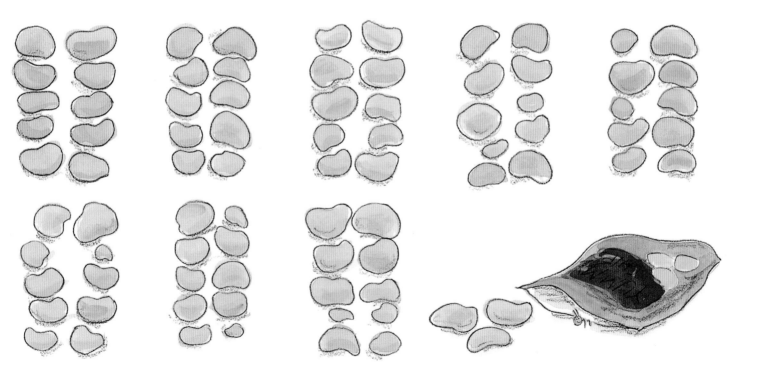

He counted **84** pieces of popcorn,

and **85** ants.

There were lots of tasty treats at the bake sale, and George had saved just enough room for dessert. What treat should he pick?

There were **86** cupcakes,

How many cherries
can you find?

How many
cupcakes
does George
have on
his head?

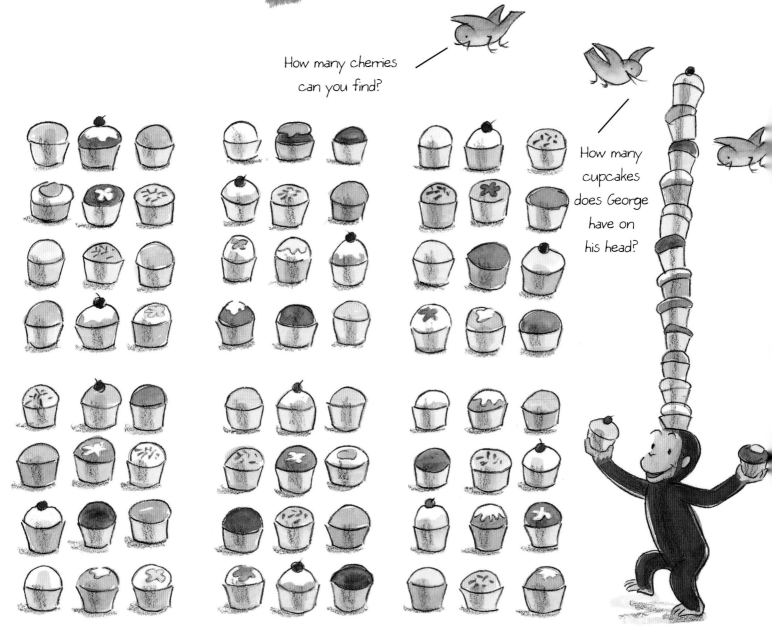

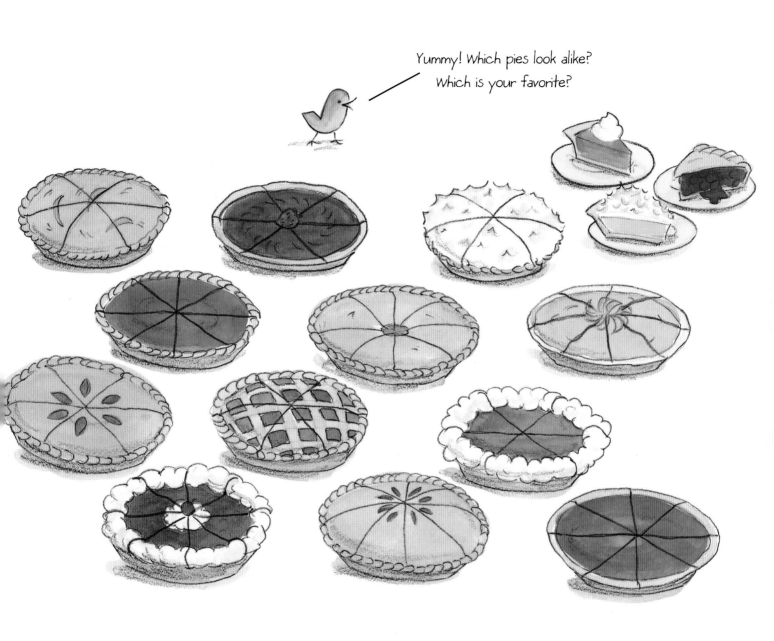

and **87** slices of pie.

While George ate just one of the **88** cookies, he remembered what he wanted to see next . . .

The games!

George and Olivia took turns throwing balls at **89** holes.

Bull's eye!

Olivia scored and George helped her choose one of the **90** prizes.

Good aim!

Swing, swing, swing, pop! One of the games was a piñata. George arrived just in time—the paper pig broke, and **91** candies spilled out!

Uh, oh

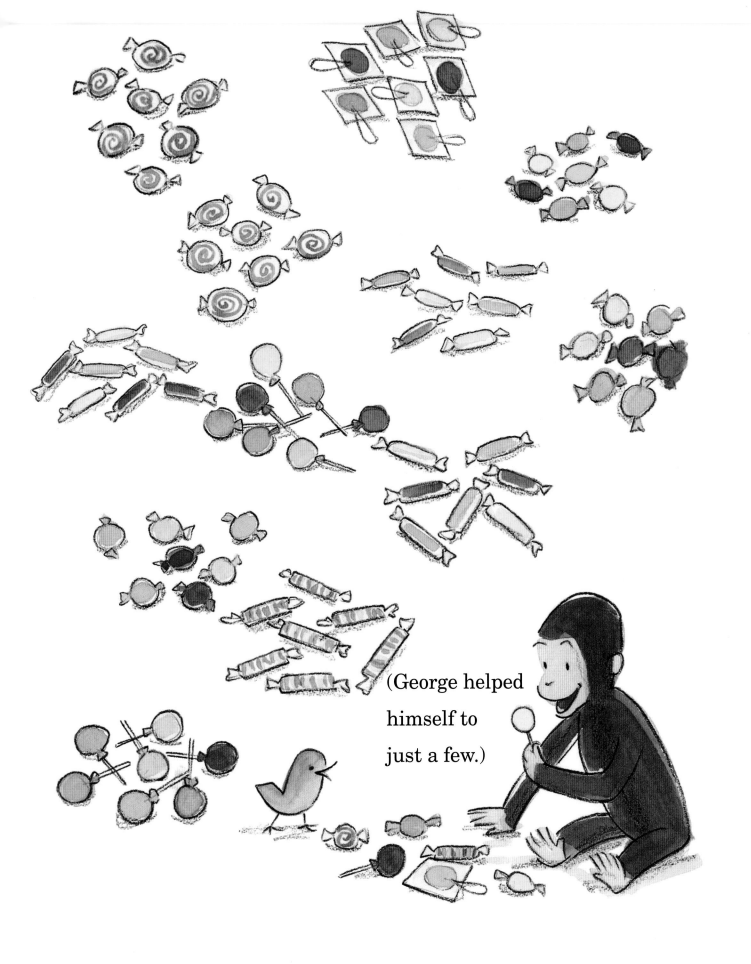

(George helped
himself to
just a few.)

Then George went to help his neighbor, Mrs. Needleman.
"Hello, George!" she called from her flower cart. "Your
friend told me you are trying to count to one hundred. Can
you count my flowers for me? I've sold a lot today, but I
think I have close to one hundred left."

Mrs. Needleman was right! George counted **92** flowers still in her cart. Then Mrs. Needleman had an idea . . .

"George," she asked, "can you help me count the money I made today?" The Centennial Celebration was almost over, and Mrs. Needleman had to organize her money to bring it to the bank.

Together they stacked **93** nickels,

94 quarters,

95 pennies,

96 dimes,

Look at the coins like a detective. Which is biggest? Which is smallest? Which coins have smooth edges?

and **97** dollars. Mrs. Needleman helped George count. He was even closer to one hundred, but he wasn't there yet!

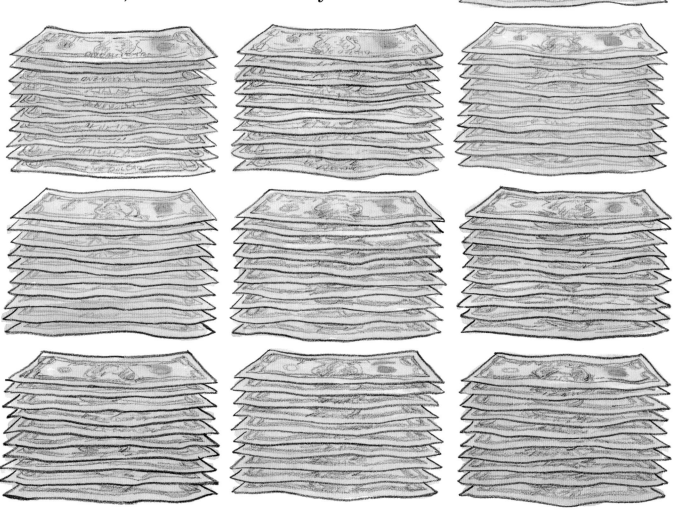

Mrs. Needleman pointed to where some children were playing. "Maybe they can help you reach one hundred, George," she said, then gave him a flower to thank him for his help. "Good luck, George!"

Some kids were playing sidewalk games. And Betsy was with them!
"You've been counting all day, George," she said. "You must be almost
to one hundred. Keep going!"

George counted ██ marbles

and **99** jacks.

He was so close to one hundred!
He only needed one more thing to
count—but what would it be?

And then George knew
just what to do.

Just one more,
George!

Go, George!

George ran and ran. He ran 100 steps—all the way back to the man with the yellow hat!

His friend was so happy to see him. "You did it, George!" his friend said proudly. "You used your own two feet to count all the way to one hundred! What a perfect way to end a centennial day."

George was proud too, and after his very full day, he was happy to be with his friend—the person he counted on most.

The End!

YOUNG CHILDREN, NUMBERS, AND COUNTING

Reading and exploring *Curious George Learns to Count* with your child offers many possibilities for enhancing your child's sense of numbers. Goals for preschool children are to count by rote to twenty, to count up to twenty objects accurately, and to recognize numbers up to twenty. Kindergartners and first-graders are learning to count to one hundred, to count up to one hundred objects accurately, and to recognize numbers up to one hundred. First-graders are working on counting by twos, fives, and tens. Practicing counting is valuable for young children of any age and will help build their understanding of the relationships between numbers.

As you open this book again and again, here are some things to think about:

- Your child can enjoy the story without counting every object that George counts. Your child will hear the numbers increase as the story progresses.

- Ask questions that allow your child to think about the numbers. You might ask what the highest or lowest number is on a page. What number will be on the next page?

- Offer support by counting together and model counting as you read. You can use your finger to count a group of objects one by one. You can also hold your child's hand and point at the objects together as you count.

- Some groups of objects are more challenging to count than others. You can show your child how to put small markers (pennies or torn pieces of paper) on the objects as they are counted. Your child can use this strategy in other tricky counting situations.

**Here are some ideas for exploring numbers in your child's world
the way George does in his:**

- Guess My Number. To play this game, think of a number in the range your child is learning. Tell your child that the number is between one and ten (for very young children) or between one and one hundred (for older children). Each time your child guesses a number respond with "higher" or "lower" until your number is guessed. Eventually, you can take turns being the guesser.

- Number Search. Take a walk in your neighborhood to look for numbers. Don't worry if your child says "seven two" for seventy-two. You can respond with something like "Yes, I see seventy-two also." While acknowledging your child's observation, you're also providing the correct way of reading the number.

- Walking Count. Another walk involves counting the steps you take from one place to another. Or you can select something specific to count—sidewalk squares, or, like George, houses or trees.

- Count Around the House. What can your child count in your home that George counted in his? Do you have more or less of these than George did?

- Skip Counting. Take any opportunity to group by twos, fives, and tens. For example, you can deal the cards by twos if you're playing a card game with your child.

- Laundry Count. Your child can help sort the clean laundry. He or she can be in charge of matching (also an important skill) the socks and then counting them by twos.

There are so many ways to enrich your child's world with numbers and counting
Explore, enjoy, and watch your child learn to count with
Curious George—a perfect learning companion.

1 2 3 4 5 6 7 8 9 10 11
12 13 14 15 16 17 18 19 20
21 22 23 24 25 26 27 28
29 30 31 32 33 34 35 36
37 38 39 40 41 42 43 44
45 46 47 48 49 50 51 52
53 54 55 56 57 58 59 60
61 62 63 64 65 66 67 69
70 71 72 73 74 76 77 78
79 80 81 82 85 86
87 88 89 90 94
95 96 97 98 99 100